COBA

TEXT
Archeologist María Jose Con

TITLE PAGE
Nohoch Mul

HALF TITLE
Stela 20
Tlaoli Ramírez

PHOTOGRAPHS
Adalberto Rios
Dagli Orti
David Stuart (p. 35)
Monclem Archives

TRANSLATION:
Nicholas Papworth

CONACULTA · INAH
Reproduction authorized by the National
Institute of Archaeology and History

© 2007, Monclem Ediciones S.A. de C.V.
Leibnitz 31, colonia Anzures 11590
México, D.F.
www.monclem.com
e-mail: monclem@monclem.com
Tels.: 55 45 07 39 • 52 55 42 48
ISBN 978-970-9019-44-5

Printed in Mexico
Stellar Group, S.A. de C.V.
E. Rébsamen 314 y 315, Narvarte
03020, México, D.F.
February, 2010

Index

Maya Culture

▶ Temple of the Sun at Palenque. Representative example of Palenque architecture: mansard roofs with cresting, decorated with personages and animals fashioned in stucco. In the interior is a carved panel with a solar disc and the figures of two of Palenque's principal rulers.

Maya civilization is one of the most important in the history of humanity and forms part of a broader cultural area: Mesoamerica, with which it shared many traits. In cultural terms, the territory defined as the Maya area according to archaeological vestiges and modern speakers of the Maya language, is limited by the present-day borders of the Yucatan Peninsula, practically the whole of the states of Chiapas and Tabasco in Mexico, together with Guatemala, Belize and El Salvador, as well as the eastern portion of Honduras.

The area's vast size includes the most varied types of environment: mountainous highlands, fertile valleys, lowlands and coastal plains, as well as a wide variety of flora, fauna and climates, from cool or warm to humid or dry. Such a variety of landscapes is likewise accompanied by a rich multiplicity of local cultural manifestations.

Maya culture cannot be viewed in terms of isolated development. Its origins date back to 2500 B.C., when groups of farmers began to settle in the region. The first major phase in Mesoamerican cultural history was the Pre-Classic (1500 B.C. to 300 A.D.), which pertains to the emergence of civilization in Mesoamerica. In the early stages, around 1200 B.C., one of the

first major civilizations emerged in southern Veracruz: the Olmec, actually considered the mother of many of the Mesoamerican cultures, among them the Maya. During the period from 300 B.C. to 300 A.D., the Maya built urban centers with large populations ruled by elite groups. They erected large-scale buildings, sculpted stelae with images of the rulers and registered dynastic successions using the long-count system.

◀ The skill of Maya sculptors is reflected in Yaxchilán's Lintel 53, which represents a Shield-Jaguar I holding a scepter-mannequin before Lady *Ik'*-Cráneo (Skull), who is holding a bundle with implements used for self-sacrifice.

▶ The scenes depicted on ceramic objects have made it possible for us to become familiar with the history, cosmogony, mythology and court life of the Maya. These vessels were used to serve food at important celebrations and funeral offerings. Tikal, Guatemala.

During the Classic period (300–900 A.D.), Maya culture reached its peak in virtually every field: art, architecture, science, the stelae cult and hieroglyphic writing. Relations between the different cities during this period were established primarily by trading goods and by alliances between the rulers, sometimes cemented by marriage ties. Towards the end of the 8th century some of the main cities experienced a rapid population decline, and the political power weakened. There is no single reason in particular to explain this; perhaps the most plausible answer is to attribute the eclipse of the Classic to a number of concurrent factors, such as droughts, wars and political upheavals. The Post-Classic (900 – 1521 A.D.) was a period of migrations and influences from other cultural groups, most of them from Central Mexico. Furthermore, a coasting trade network developed along the Maya seashore, stretching from the Gulf of Mexico as far as Honduras.

In addition to their skills as architects and artists, among this culture's most notable intellectual achievements was their knowledge of astronomy, the computation of time, and hieroglyphic writing. As keen and accurate observers of the heavens, they calculated the solstices and equinoxes and the cycle of Venus at 584 days, predicted eclipses of the sun and moon and made observations of the planets and constellations.

The Maya devised various ways of measuring time; the cycles they used were the *tzolkin*, the *haab*, the Long Count, the Lord of the Night and the age of the Moon. The *tzolkin* or Sacred Count was a 260-day cycle of a ritual and divinatory nature. The *haab* was composed of a solar year of 365 days, consisting of eighteen 20-day months. Both calendars coincided every 52 years. To quantify lineal time they recurred to the Long Count, which began on the date of the third creation, that is, August 13, 3114 B.C., as of which the time elapsed was counted on the basis of a 360-day year called *tun*.

CHRONOLOGICAL TABLE		
YEARS	**PERIODS**	**CHARACTERISTICS**
1500 B.C.	Early Pre-Classic	Villages' cultural development and burgeoning population gave rise to large-scale settlements governed by elite groups. The constructions highlighted the importance of such cities and reinforced acceptance of the rulers' power. Also, stelae computed according to the Long Count showing images of rulers performing rituals began to appear.
900 B.C.	Middle Pre-Classic	
300 B.C.	Late Pre-Classic	
250 A.D.	Early Clasic	The Classic period saw the flowering of art and architecture and elite cultural expressions such as stelae worship, iconography of kinship and hieroglyphic writing. Towards the end of the period many cities in the southern lowlands were abandoned, while those in the north of the peninsula survived for a few centuries longer.
900 A.D.	Late Classic	
1100 A.D.	Early Post-Classic	In the Post-Classic period, migrations from central Mexico caused radical changes. A coasting trade route was established from the Gulf of Mexico to Honduras. New architectural styles were developed and their cosmic vision of the world changed.
1200 A.D.	Late Post-Classic	
1521 A.D.	Conquest	The Maya continued worshipping the same deities. This, together with the practice of human sacrifice, made the Spaniards destroy all artistic representations so as to eradicate these age-old beliefs.

▲ Dresden Codex. Of religious and ritual content, the work deals with the periods of Venus and the prediction of solar and lunar eclipses. Glyphs and numerals made up of dots and bars are painted there, as well as representations of gods and priests.

Furthermore, Maya hieroglyphic writing was a system made up of the combination of three different types of signs: logographic (representation of words), phonetic (representation of sounds) and semantic (representation of meanings). Their writings were depicted on architecture, sculpture, painting, ceramics, ornamental and ritual objects and on books made of tree bark or deerskin and painted – the so-called codices, of which only three survive.

The rulers, who were considered descendants of the deities, used to celebrate rituals of self-sacrifice and this legitimized them and allowed them to communicate with their ancestors. Another common practice was sacrificing captives.

Coba through time

▶ This is the first known photographic image of the upper temple of Nohoch Mul. It was taken in 1891 by German explorer Teobert Maler during a brief visit to the site. One of the three niches with the descending god on the façade of the building had collapsed.

Coba is located north-east of the Yucatan Peninsula, in the north of the state of Quintana Roo, 28 miles west of the Caribbean coast. It is perhaps the largest Pre-Hispanic settlement of the Classic period in northern Yucatan. It is situated between lagoons and a rich vegetation whose variety of trees, shrubs and thickets were used at some time by the ancient Maya for building wooden houses and lintels for the temples and for gathering aromatic resins, fruits and edible seeds, as well as medicinal remedies. Among the most important of these are ramón, cedar, mahogany, zapote (from which chicle gum is extracted) and huano, a kind of palm used for thatched roofs. The fauna now inhabiting this region is much scarcer than in ancient times, due, among other reasons, to population growth, deforestation and hunting. Coba is nevertheless a kind of refuge for certain animals, such as deer, badger, armadillo, mountain hog, skunk, various types of snakes and many species of birds (partridge, chachalaca, parrot, mountain turkey, etc.). The lagoons were populated by crocodiles and certain species of fish. It was still possible to see the occasional jaguar some twenty years ago.

Coba is the site's original name, as attested to by some of the inscriptions found at the site, but its meaning is uncertain; some believe it means "choppy water" in reference to the lagoons.

The history of Coba's development over the centuries, from its beginnings to its complete abandonment, is still undergoing intensive research. So far there is only a rough outline of its evolution and its relation to other sites. On the other hand, the almost total absence of sources of surface water made the lagoons the determining factor in Coba's being established at that site.

The oldest evidence of a settlement at Coba dates back to the Late Pre-Classic period and this is attested to by fragments of ceramic pieces dated between 100 B.C. and 200 A.D. It may be conjectured that during this early stage the groups were made up of villages established close to the lakes whose economy was based above all on agriculture and hunting. Thus far no buildings dating from this period have been found. The Classic began with the centralization of economic and political power and control was already exercised over nearby settlements joined by *sacbeoob* or white roads. Coba's development as an urban center began during the Early Classic (250-600 A.D.) and in the Middle Classic it became a regional capital interconnected with the Petén

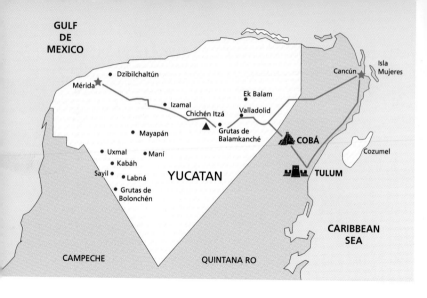

area. Towards the end of the Classic (800–1000 A.D.), building activities reached a peak, relations with the Petén declined, and increased with the Gulf Coast.

The Classic period includes numerous architectural remains, almost all with a well-defined structure and orientation: raised platforms with vaulted rooms forming plazas and patios. The altars or benches within the rooms seem to be related to buildings of a later era, and likewise the struts on the staircases. The masonry is based on regularly faced limestone with stucco covering, with or without chromatic ornamentation. It is common to find traces of modeled, painted stucco decoration of the friezes and façades, and sometimes, mural paintings within the rooms. In the Early Post-Classic (1000-1250 A.D.) Coba was affected by the invasion or influence of the *Itzaes*, who probably converted it into a civic-ceremonial center. There was a marked decline in architectural activity and the constructions acquired more "Mexicanized" traits, with a type of architecture similar to that found in Mayapán and the east coast of the peninsula, at places such as Xcaret, Xelhá, Tancah and Tulum. During this period the foundations of major constructions from earlier times were used to superimpose other new ones. The buildings were of smaller dimensions, with cruder masonry, drawn-in lintels, interior footways and altars and struts on the stairways; this set of architectural features was known as the "East coast style". In the Late Post-Classic (1250-1450 A.D.) Coba's power weakened and it received strong influences from Mayapán and east-coast groups. As of that time, Coba perhaps became a center of pilgrimage or cult for coastal or inland groups; by this time the city must have been sparsely inhabited.

In 1842 the traveler John L. Stephens, accompanied by the fine English draughtsman Frederick Catherwood, traveled through much of the Yucatan Peninsula, Chiapas and Central America. It is to him that the first reference of the existence of the ruins of Coba is due. Stephens, who never reached the area, knew of its existence from some notes compiled by a priest from Chemax which alluded to buildings and a paved road. The War of Castes, which began in 1847 in Yucatan, made it dangerous and practically impossible for visitors to enter the area during those years. In 1882 Yucatecan intellectual Juan Peón Contreras visited Coba and made drawings of some of the main structures. German archaeologist Teobert Maler made a short visit in 1891 and his observations include a few notes in which he briefly described certain buildings in the Coba and Nohoch Mul groups, some of the stelae and *sacbé 1*, and took the first known photograph of the upper building of Nohoch Mul. Rafael Regil, a friend of Maler's, visited the site in 1897. In 1926 Thomas Gann made a brief visit and described several buildings of the Nohoch Mul group, a few stelae and walked along *sacbé 1* for about 16 miles. Excited by what he saw at the site, Gann gave an account of it to the archaeologists of the *Carnegie Institution* in Washington, who at that time were exploring Chichén Itzá. His descriptions aroused immediate interest, and it was then that the *Carnegie* organized several expeditions culminating in 1930. The publication in 1932 of the first formal research papers on Coba, carried out by J. Eric S. Thompson, Harry E. D. Pollock and Jean Charlot were the product of six expeditions in which Alfred D. Kidder and Sylvanus G. Morley also took part. Around that time, Alfonso Villa Rojas traveled the length of *sacbé 1* and described its 100 km course. Forty years after the research done by Thompson, Pollock and Charlot, Mexico's National Institute of Anthropology and History continues its explorations in Coba.

Characteristics of Coba

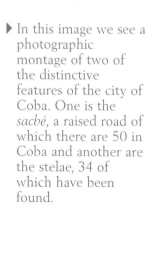

▶ In this image we see a photographic montage of two of the distinctive features of the city of Coba. One is the *sacbé*, a raised road of which there are 50 in Coba and another are the stelae, 34 of which have been found.

The sacbé

One of Coba's distinctive features is undoubtedly a network of roads leading north, south, east and west; thus, the city had internal communication as well as intercommunication with neighboring sites and even distant regions. Since the wheel was unknown and there were no animals of burden or draft, these roads made it easier for people and the goods carried –whether traded items or tributes– to move more quickly through the jungle. These white roads were called *sacbé* in Yucatecan Maya or, in the plural, *sacbeoob* (*sac*, white; *be*, road). These communication routes had different lengths, heights, widths and functions. Their height above the ground depends on the terrain's natural contours, which are most irregular in this region. Consequently, one of them has side walls reaching 16 and 19 feet in height. So far just over 50 *sacbeoob* have been located in Coba, but only 45 of them have been registered in detail. The longest is *sacbé 1*, measuring 62 miles, which reaches as far as Yaxuná, an archaeological site near Chichén Itzá.

The stelae

Another of the site's features are the 34 sculpted stelae dating from the Classic period and a lesser number of plain ones; perhaps because the latter were not sculpted, they were covered with stucco and painted.

The stelae are situated near the buildings or on them. They consist of large blocks of limestone sculpted in bas-relief, placed vertically and on their own. They depicted the images and names of certain rulers and also recorded important historical events: births, marriages, deaths, ascents to power, conquests, as well as significant astronomical happenings. Exposure to the elements for hundreds of years and the nature of the limestone used –not very hard and highly soluble– have led to a marked erosion of these monuments. This has made it virtually impossible to read dates on the stelae except on just a few, during a period between 613 and 780 A.D. Unfortunately, important testimonies that would supply invaluable historical information on Coba have been wiped out by the passage of time. In the main, the stelae of Coba show very similar subject-matter, even though each

15

one makes reference to different events and facts. The left side of the monument, from top to bottom, displays columns of glyphs. In the center is the main personage, shown facing the front, the feet open to the sides and the face turned towards the observer's left. The figure is decked out in sumptuous finery and is adorned with necklaces, bracelets, belt and an elaborate headdress. The arms hold a great ruler's scepter across the chest. These main personages are accompanied by captives who sometimes serve them as pedestals or may be kneeling or in an attitude of supplication beside them. Their wrists or arms are always tied and sometimes the feet, too. One thing that is very much apparent is the contrast between the excessive rigidity, solemnity and elegance of the main figure and the body movement, expressiveness and simplicity of dress of the captives. Near the slaves we see the glyphs identifying them. Some stelae were moved from their original position and were placed as a whole or just some of their fragments on buildings, staircases or patios; this was a recurrent practice. During the Post-Classic period, simple shrines with low walls on three sides were built around some of them. In some cases they were accompanied by round altars belonging to the Classic period, as with stelae 1, 3, 5, 6 and 8 of the Macanxoc group and 11 of the Coba group. During the Post-Classic period, very rudimentary small square altars were placed before them, as exemplified by stelae 3, 4, 5 and 8 of the Macanxoc group. This leads us to believe that there was continuity in the veneration of the stelae over a long period of time, to the extent that even today some of the stelae at Coba are cult objects for the inhabitants of the community, who consider them, among other things, as the guardians of the jungle. The oral traditions transmitted by modern settlers over the years recount that the stelae are ancient kings who turn to stone in the daytime and come to life at night.

Modeled stucco and mural painting

In Coba, as at almost any archeological site, the original buildings were not as we see them today. In fact, all the constructions were covered both inside and out by a white stucco finish or plaster, which on occasions was painted red. The Maya placed great care on decoration, which was not only used to decorate the buildings, but the motifs represented could also have religious or political significance, depending on the function of each building. Moreover, the façades were often decorated with modeled stucco in high relief and painted in different colors. The themes were naturalist and figurative, with human or animal faces, deities, glyphs, etc. Another type of decoration used was mural painting to represent scenes alluding to political and religious life. During the Classic period mural painting was used particularly on the inside of buildings, whereas in the Post-Classic it was used in both interiors and exteriors.

Map of Coba

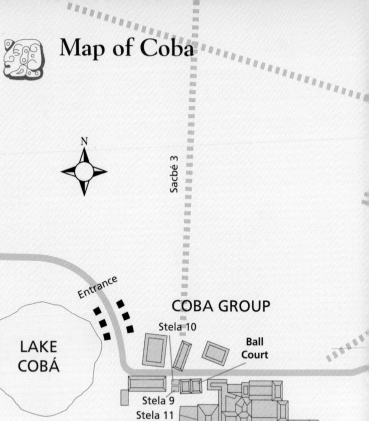

N

Sacbé 3

Entrance

COBA GROUP

LAKE COBÁ

Stela 10

Ball Court

Stela 9

Stela 11

The Church

Structure 4

LAKE MACANXOC

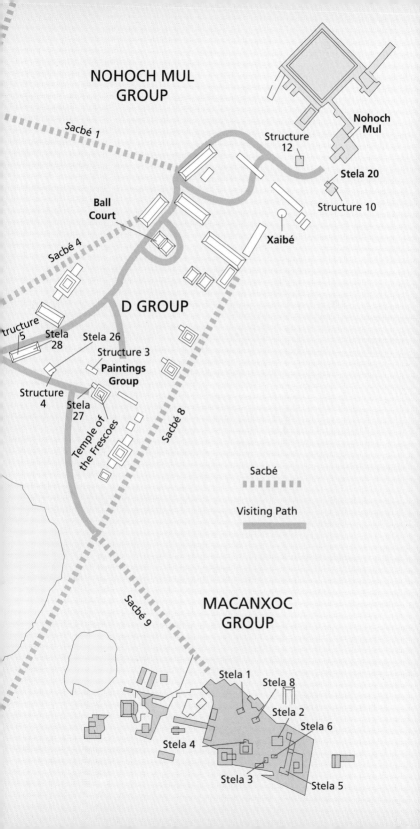

NOHOCH MUL GROUP

Sacbé 1

Structure 12

Nohoch Mul

Stela 20

Structure 10

Ball Court

Sacbé 4

Xaibé

D GROUP

Structure 5

Stela 28

Stela 26

Structure 3

Paintings Group

Structure 4

Stela 27

Temple of the Frescoes

Sacbé 8

Sacbé

Visiting Path

Sacbé 9

MACANXOC GROUP

Stela 1

Stela 8

Stela 2

Stela 6

Stela 4

Stela 3

Stela 5

 # Monuments and art in Coba

Coba Group

Located between the Coba and Macanxoc lakes, this great set of 53 buildings is the most ancient in the entire city and it is where some *sacbeoob* begin, setting off in various directions. It has an acropolis with a number of buildings and multiple superimpositions which emphasize the significance of this

series of buildings, which were used for hundreds of years and were the city's most important for a long period of time. Only a small portion of this major collection of buildings has been explored and may be visited. A long set of stands leading to a vaulted staircase provides access to two patios surrounded by buildings in which one of the site's principal constructions stands. These stands may have been used as seats to witness important events in the main plaza. Their steps were decorated in modeled stucco and painted in vivid colors.

▶ The Church

This was previously known as "The Castle"; it is likely that its current name of "The Church" is due to the fact that the stela situated at the foot continues to be venerated. Seventy-eight feet in height and facing towards the Coba lagoon, it is the site's second tallest building. It is made up of nine rounded sections which underwent a number of alterations and additions which gradually covered and changed the original construction. The first section of the building cannot be seen, since Patio A covers it completely. Only one part of the second section is visible, since on it there are two vaulted rooms and a staircase leading to the rooms built on either side of it. Consequently, there is a platform in front of it with patios surrounded by rooms that were once vaulted and superimposed stairways that conceal the base of the Church and the rooms that were once at its sides. Construction of this building began in the Early Classic and, as a final addition, a small temple was constructed on it, which crowns the upper part. This temple, which in turn underwent a number of modifications, housed a fragment of stela and kept a rich offering from the terminal Classic, which consisted of a number of ceramic vases, beads, a jade figurine, decorated conch sections, pearls and conch pectorals.

▶ Stela 11

In the patio, at the foot of the Church and in front of the staircase is the upper fragment of a stela, surrounded by a small shrine with a circular altar before it. Although the sculpting of the stela is almost wiped out, a few glyphs can be distinguished, although not with sufficient clarity to determine the date corresponding to this monument. At present, the inhabitants of the place still venerate this stela and can distinguish a virgin they call Colebí. This deity is the object of prayers and offerings and they light candles in her honor; their prayers entrust her, among other things, with a good harvest and good luck in hunting. This practice, which was previously performed in the intimacy of a place hardly visited when the community based its subsistence on harvests and hunting, is becoming less and less frequent.

Structure 4

As part of the Acropolis of the Coba Group, and to the south of the Church, a group of buildings was erected around a raised patio, at the same level as the patio in front of the Church. These buildings, of the Late Classic period, have long parallel enclosures with entrances on opposite sides and separated by a central wall, which supported the vaults that covered them. On one side, the rooms look out over the interior of the patio and, on the other, over the great plaza of the Coba group or the patio in front of the Church. These two raised patios were communicated at some point. Due to their location within the group and their morphological characteristics, it is feasible to think that these buildings were used as rooms for the ruling class, or else as halls in which activities of a civic or administrative nature were carried out. Outstanding among them is structure 4, since it is the largest and the one that underwent the most modifications over time. Initially it was a long room with a double bay, onto which a wide stairway was superimposed, under which a vault crosses. The explorations of the room that looks out onto the plaza revealed traces, now practically disappeared, that the interior was profusely decorated with mural painting. Among the designs that were conserved, two glyphs painted black on a white background were recognized, one of them with the representation of *kaban*, which

▲ The vaulted arches under the staircases are a feature repeated in several structures in Coba. They show the manner in which the Maya arch was built.

symbolizes the earth. In front of this room, on the second step, are the remaining fragments of Stela 12. When it was first discovered in the thirties decade, it was still possible to see the main personage and the captives. The destruction it has suffered since then only allows us to appreciate the lower extremities of the squatting captive pedestal on the left and the subsidiary slaves. The three altars of different epochs that surround the stela are not oriented in relation to it. It is therefore likely that the stela was originally oriented towards the main plaza and not sideways as it is now. When the stela was placed on the stands, part of the steps were broken, which indicates that it did not correspond to its original placement. This is not the only case discovered, which means that relocation of stelae was a common practice in Coba.

Ball game (pelota)

One of Coba's two ball courts of the Late Classic lies to one side of the Acropolis. It is made up of two parallel buildings forming a passageway, which constitutes the court, which was where the game was played. On the inclined walls or slopes of each section there are built-in rectangular panels depicting naked captives, semi-kneeling and tied at the wrists, as well as a stone plaque in the center of the slope on the east side; its degree of erosion has made it impossible to determine the subject-matter depicted. In the upper central part of each slope is a ring through which the players had to pass the ball. The ball was made of rubber and could only be struck by the elbows knees or hips; these parts of the body therefore had to be properly protected.

Each building is different: the one on the east side has two

staircases, one at the back of the building and another on the north side; a vault passes underneath the latter. Both staircases lead to the upper part of the construction which has rooms, and in earlier phases was vaulted. Similarly, a series of small rooms are attached to the sides and projected towards a raised plaza to the east of the ball court. Unlike this section, the opposite one did not have a formal staircase to go up to the upper level, which must have been thatched with perishable materials such as wood and palm leaves. In the Post-Classic, long after the ball court was no longer in use, two stelae, 9 and 10, were placed within a simple shrine in the back part of this section, accompanied at the front by small square altars. Fragments of incense-burners of this period were found at the altars and, near the stelae, vestiges of ancient rites in which copal, an aromatic resin obtained from

the tree known as *pom*, was burned.

The floor of the court was covered by a very thick, compacted stucco base, which made the playing area uniform and gave the ball a good bounce. At one end, underneath the floor, a copious offering dedicated to this building was found, consisting of jade, shell and conch beads and pectorals, flint knives and awls and a small anthropomorphic sculpture made of green stone. This court had no markers on the ground, as in the Group D ball game.

The origins of the ball game in Mesoamerica go back more than 3,000 years, if we consider that it is still practiced today in some regions of Mexico. So far more than 1,500 ball courts have been found.

The ball game was of a mainly ritual nature; it was a scenario that symbolically represented the struggle between astral opposites and was also related to fertility; in other words, it was a battlefield on a symbolic plane in which occasionally human sacrifice formed an essential part. To a lesser extent, it was also a performance for entertainment. The way of playing the ball game in Mesoamerica did not follow a common pattern, but was practiced in different ways and on courts that varied in size and shape, depending on the region. For this same reason the number of players on each team was variable, as was the attire and the implements used in the game.

◀ Panel with the depiction of a captive, arms tied at the wrist. Tied to his back is the head of a jaguar with a lotus-flower bud on the forehead. The position of the figure with his wrists tied is repeated on the panels associated with Coba's two ball courts.

Kan staircase

This is situated at the far southern end of the ball game and was attached to the platform of Structure 2 of the Acropolis. It was so named for the 15 glyphs with the symbol of *kan* represented in the center and at the ends of each row of the first five steps. *Kan* in Yucatecan Maya means yellow and also refers to the southern cardinal point, although it has other meanings, such as "precious, much appreciated, necessary," for which reason it was also used to refer to the materials used in jewelry-making, for example jade, shell and bone. This symbol has also been related to corn and water, in view of its multiple links to aquatic contexts and fertility. To the sides of the staircase two representations of human skulls were built in, originally painted red and blue. In Mesoamerica, trophy heads, decapitation and skulls are related to the ball game.

Group D

This group made up of numerous structures is situated in the area formed between *sacbeoob* 4 and 8 and is limited to the north by the Nohoch Mul group and to the south by the Coba group and the Macanxoc lagoon. It is characterized by greater dispersion as regards the distribution of its structures and contains a series of buildings set out in squares and a ball court. Some constructions of the Classic period have elements added on during the Post-Classic, the last period during which Coba was occupied. This is evident from the temples, whose architecture clearly reveals an east-coast style typical of that time. Only a few structures of this extensive group have been explored and may be visited: the Paintings Group, composed of five structures and 13 altars, the Ball Court and the Xaibé.

▲ Structure 5

It forms part of the Paintings Group and consists of a building with a staircase at the front whose upper room has already lost the vault that roofed it. The sections of the structure show a variant of the Teotihuacan slope-slab and were decorated with modeled, painted stucco. Although the building belongs to the Classic period, it obviously underwent certain alterations during the Post-Classic and was reused. A room with a long stepped platform was attached to one side and Stela 28 was placed in it, whose offering consisted of four animal-shaped figurines.

◀ Structure 4

This structure is located at the center of the Paintings Group and consists of a low platform; on one of its sides Stela 26 was installed, which was incorporated into the building at a later date, most probably in the Post-Classic. In front of it is a circular stone which was part of a column, used as an altar. Apparently it belonged to the columns of Structure 3 of the same series, since its dimensions are the same.

Paintings Group

This group of ceremonial buildings was named thus due to the remains of mural painting that subsisted in two of its structures. Here we can clearly see the combination of two periods of occupation in Coba, the Classic and the Post-Classic, in which earlier buildings were reused to superimpose constructions of later periods.

Structure 1, also known as the Temple of the Frescoes, is the highest building in the entire series; its foundations, made up of four sections with rounded corners, correspond to the Late Classic period, whereas at the top is a small temple of the Post-Classic period. Both the interior and the exterior of the upper temple were at one time profusely decorated with pictorial features, but today only the decoration of the frieze is partly conserved. Moreover, of a series of glyphs, the motifs represented allude specifically to agricultural propitiatory rites linked to requests for rain. At the foot of this structure and mounted at the center of its staircase is Structure 2, whose vault is partially demolished. In the interior we can see a footway running parallel to the walls and surrounding a fragment of Stela 27. Structure 3, for its part, is a long, open enclosure with two rows of seven columns with square capitals which probably supported roofing made of wood and palm leaves. Sufficient data are not available to be able to deduce the function this structure; nonetheless, its close relationship with the 13 small altars in

front of it has led to the conclusion that it was closely connected to the religious rites held there. The group of small altars in front of structures 2 and 3 served to place incense-burners used in ceremonies, as shown by the numerous fragments found. To one side of the little altars a cist can be seen where a burial was deposited. Both Structure 3 and the altars and the cist date from the Post-Classic period.

Ball court

This is comparable in form and time with the ball court of the Coba group. They share similar features, such as the panels with semi-kneeling captives tied at the wrists that were placed on the slopes, and the ring on each section. Certain elements that distinguish them should be underscored; in this case, for example, the rings are sculpted with the symbol of Venus, a planet that the Maya of the Classic period linked to death, sacrifice and war. In contrast to the other ball court, this court has two markers, a central one with the representation in stone of a human skull, beside which an offering was found and, at one end, a round disc showing a decapitated jaguar, sitting in profile with the tail upright. It is believed that the markers on the court were used as a reference for scoring points in the game. Both ball courts show allusions to death in the form of human skulls, that is, death by decapitation linked to the ball game.

Stone Plaques on the Ball Court

A great hieroglyphic stone plaque was placed in the center of the slope of the north section. It contains 74 glyph capsules whose calligraphic style indicates that it was probably sculpted during the Late Classic (600-900 A.D.). It registers retrospectively historical events of the local dynasty that took place during the Early Classic. It tells that around June 5, 465 A.D. a local ruler with the title of *Kalo 'mte'*, one of the most distinguished positions in the dynasties of the Maya Classic, celebrated the end of a 10-year cycle, and that 108 days later, on October 21, 465 A.D., another dignitary with the title of *Kalo 'mte' Ahaw* dedicated a stone monument in the ball game. A third register alludes to the construction of the ball court in *Kob'a'*, an earlier place-name for the site.

Replicas of two more stone slabs are to one side of the building, but their original place is unknown, although they were almost certainly on the slopes. One of them represents a ball player holding a cross-shaped object. To one side of the ball court we can see one of the ends of *sacbé 4*, which either arrived at or started from this point.

▼ Sacbé 1

In the direction of the Nohoch Mul group you go past one side of the start of *sacbé 1*, the longest of all the ones found in Coba. This road is 62 miles long with an average height of 30 inches and a width of 32 feet. It runs northwest to Yaxuná, an ancient Maya city a few miles from Chichén Itzá. The manner of construction of the *sacbeoob* was no different from that used in other constructions in the city. They are formed by two vertical walls of roughly-shaped stone filled with loose stone and smaller stones on top mixed with earth and mortar. The entire road was finished with a thick layer of stucco. Close to mile 40 an enormous stone roller was found which was used as a leveler to flatten the road. Its path crosses with *sacbeoob* 19, 2 and 3 and has *sacbé* 43 as a branch road. The crossing of *sacbeoob* 1 and 3, roughly half a mile from its starting point, has ramps on all four sides. All along the way a number of pre-Hispanic sites were spotted along the roadside, as well as abandoned haciendas and six stones inscribed with hieroglyphics.

▲ Xaibé

In Maya, *Xaibé* means "road crossing"; the archaeologists gave it that name because *sacbeoob* 1, 5, 6 and 8 converge near this building. Its shape is not very conventional in Maya architecture: it has an apsidal floor and five rounded sections with sloping walls finished with a cornice. As can be seen, there was no temple on the upper part. It has a staircase that splits into two parts: one of normal dimensions which was added later to the building and which reaches the beginning of the second section. The original "staircase" is turned in and is visible from the second section; nevertheless, its proportions suggest that it would be difficult to fulfill that function. The building belongs to the Classic, but during the Post-Classic a fragment of Stela 31 was placed at the foot of the staircase, delimited by two low walls. A stone sculpture of a serpent's head was placed in front of the stela as an offering and underneath it an offering of marine elements. Although the tendency is to consider all round buildings astronomical observatories, there is no evidence whatsoever to support this notion in the case of this monument, and nor has its purpose been clarified.

Nohoch Mul Group

The words *Nohoch Mul* come from the Maya *nohoch* (big) and *mul* (mound), clearly referring to the group's main structure. This group consists of various buildings forming part of a great plaza showing a pronounced drop towards the south. The number of buildings that compose it is not very numerous, although it has the structures with the largest volume in the entire site, for example an impressive platform, so far unexplored, to one side of the Nohoch Mul building which is 110 yards long per side. Only three buildings in this group can be visited.

The Nohoch Mul

This imposing building measures 138 feet in height and is the tallest in the entire Yucatan Peninsula. It has seven sections with rounded and turned-in corners, common in the architecture of the Classic period in Coba. It has a wide central stairway which splits into two almost on arriving at the cusp, thus providing access to a platform where there is a temple, a later addition to the original base erected during the Post-Classic period. The molding of the niches have representations in stucco of a descending deity, with remains of blue and red paint. To one side of the main stairway is another stairway leading to a vaulted room in whose interior a fragment of stela sculpted on both sides is conserved. On the other side of the main stairway two adjacent rooms were built at different levels from the base; one is at ground level and the other at the height of the first section. From the upper part, if we look carefully, it is possible to see the Xaibé and beyond, various buildings rising above the plant canopy which are groups of edifices of the ancient city.

▼ Structure 10

This is located in the great plaza of the Nohoch Mul Group. It consists of a low platform with rounded corners, the upper part of which supports a precinct consisting of two rooms whose vault did not resist the passage of time. The first room has seven entrances, and access to the second is only possible through the first. To position Stela 20, the stairway providing access to the structure was broken in the middle, so clearly this building was not initially thought of as a place to accommodate it. So far, this stela is the best preserved of all the ones found, due particularly to the fact that when it broke and fell it remained upside-down, thus protecting it to a certain extent from the elements. The date registered on it (November 30, 780 A.D.) is the most recent inscribed on carved monuments recovered to date in Coba. This is important, since it indicates the time when, for reasons not yet known, stelae ceased to be erected on the site.

The stela shows a personage wearing elegant attire, holding a great ceremonial or ruler's scepter in his arms. His feet rest on the backs of two prostrate captives tied with ropes. Another two subsidiary slaves are also tied and kneeling on either side of them. The plinth on which the stela rests is modern and its purpose is to avoid deterioration from the accumulation of rainwater.

Structure 12

In the same plaza and almost in front of Structure 10 is this small platform with sloping walls. It is similar to Structure 4 of the Paintings Group and both have stelae placed during a second stage of occupation of the building. In this case, Stela 21 blocked the main access. Inside this platform a second vaulted precinct was found, possibly prepared as a tomb. Nevertheless, only a small offering was discovered, without any human remains. The passage of time has almost completely worn away the sculpted motifs and it is only possible to recognize certain details on the lower part. The descriptions made by the first explorers of the site show that the subject-matter represented was the usual type found in the majority of Coba's stelae.

Macanxoc Group

If you walk along *sacbé* 9 (it is 65 feet wide, that is, the widest in the whole of Coba) you reach this group of buildings. On the walk along the *sacbé* you come across a plain stela and round altars. In view of the width of this road it has been thought that there must have been a considerable flow of people, highlighting the importance this group must have had. The buildings are situated on a large artificial terrace which rises between 3 and 13 feet above the surface, that is, at a level higher than that of the *sacbé*. Almost certainly there were steps at the end of the *sacbé* in order to come out onto the main square, but explorations have not yet been carried out at this point.

In this group we can see structures of considerable volume and height, as well as low platforms and simple shrines. It is most likely that the function of the buildings in this group was purely ceremonial, since no enclosed areas have been found to enable their use as dwellings. Macanxoc gathers together the largest number of stelae in the entire site (eight in all) and has 18 altars, almost all of them related to the stelae. Despite the stelae's marked degree of erosion, you can see them more clearly if you are fortunate enough to be there at the time of day when the light is most favorable for highlighting the figures. The themes of the Macanxoc stelae does not differ from those of other groups. The central personage is richly decked out, holds a great scepter across his chest and captives lie at his feet and to the sides. These monuments relate the history of their rulers and commemorate some important happening. The dates on the stelae differ by some 10 years, which the Maya considered a *lahuntun*, which was sometimes commemorated by the erection of stelae.

▲ Stela 1

This stela is placed within a simple precinct, open on opposite sides, in the upper part of Structure 9, which is a platform with stairways on all four sides. Undoubtedly used for ceremonial purposes, two large monolithic altars were placed, facing each side of the stela. It is one of the few stelae that was sculpted in all four sides; it has 313 glyphs, and its singularity lies in the fact that it has four dates of the Long Count, a unique case so far in the entire Maya area. The four dates signal events that took place in the seventh century: three of them refer to past episodes that took place on January 29, 653, June 29, 672 and August 28, 682 A.D.; the fourth alludes to a future winter solstice, December 21, 2012.

▼ Stela 4

This is located within a small vaulted sanctuary and placed at the base of the stairway of Structure 2, one of Macanxoc's tallest buildings. The staircase at the front is wide, but only a few steps have been explored. The staircase leads to a landing; from that point, another small staircase leads to the upper part where the remains of a temple can be found. The sanctuary protecting the stela is a small, narrow vaulted room which is partly in ruins. Initially, the staircase was whole, and at some point it was sectioned to add the sanctuary and the stela. Two elements lead us to believe that the stela was first situated in a place different from the present one: first, the break in the staircase to build the sanctuary where the stela was introduced and second, the objects offered up were so simple that it could hardly be thought that they pertained to a monument of that category. Of the entire scene depicted, what can be seen most clearly are the two captives under the feet of the main personage. In the text, made up of 132 glyphs, the date recorded is March 19, 623 A.D., which corresponds to a spring equinox.

▲ Stela 8

Within Structure 8 and placed at the center and against the back wall of this ample sanctuary we can see the lower segment of Stela 8, the only fragment preserved. Beside it an offering from this same period was found, consisting of shell and jade beads. Although not clearly visible, the stela has the characteristic representation found on other stelae; in this case the main personage places his feet on two captives while another two captives kneel on either side. The date inscribed is October 12, 652 A.D. In front of the sanctuary there are some small square altars used in the ceremonial rites that took place. In the structure where stelae 1 and 8 are located, another round monolithic altar can be found.

▲ Stela 3

This stela is situated in front of Structure 6, a building that underwent several construction stages. The oldest is a small temple with entrances on all four sides whose dimensions indicate that it had an exclusively ceremonial purpose. The walls were painted orange and red. The roof was in all probability a vault of fairly rudimentary construction. Subsequently, the structure was covered by two more constructions now partly removed, the last of these corresponding to the frontal footways where the stela now stands. Before it are two altars, a round one on which a flint knife was found and another altar, smaller and square, which dates from the Post-Classic, the last period of occupation of Coba. The stela is carved on only one of its sides and has 160 blocks of glyphs set out in nine columns. The sculpting style is of a earlier artistic stage, since in comparison with the other stelae the depiction appears to be more rudimentary. The date inscribed is January 25, 633 A.D.

Stela 2

Leaning against what appears to be the center of the staircase of Structure 7, is Stela 2. In this case, the stela shows the central personage standing on the back of a single captive with his hands tied and lying face down, a unique example in the stelae found. In front of it we find a square altar belonging to the Late Classic, as well as an oval cist from the Post-Classic. The date inscribed on this monument is December 4, 642 A.D.

Stela 5

This is at the foot of the stairway of Structure 3 and, like Stela 4, is sculpted on all four sides; the front and back depict high-ranking personages, slaves and glyphs, whereas the sides have only glyphs. Its advanced deterioration only enables us to conjecture than the number of glyphs is 55 on one side and 68 on the other. The monument has been approximately dated August 21, 662 A.D. Linked to the stela is a circular altar of the Classic period and next to it, a cist with a few fragments of human bones. A small square altar of the Post-Classic period is also situated near the stela.

Stela 6

Stela 6 is located within a small sanctuary in front of a set of buildings of considerable size. It has 49 blocks of glyphs set out in eight columns. It is sculpted only on one side and depicts a personage holding the ruler's or ceremonial scepter against his chest and with a tied, kneeling captive to one side. The date inscribed on this monument is the oldest registered on the stelae of Coba, May 10, 613 A.D. No other stela of those explored has had an offering as rich as this one. In particular, the material recovered included decorated shell and conch earrings, jade beads and plaques with representations of gods, and flint and pyrite objects. Found to one side of the sanctuary were the remains of a monolithic circular altar, which had probably been in front of the stela.

Discover
Mexico
in full color

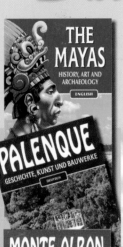

Our guides will help you get to know all about Mexico's archaeological, historical, artistic and cultural wealth.

Did you know that the Maya established trade routes, that their gods were symbolized in the shape of animals and that they created two calendars, a solar one and a ritual one?

You will find all this information and much more in the different titles we have available in several languages.